I CHOOSE ME
Taking The Stand To Make It All About Me!

Tosha S. Anderson D. Min

ANEW POINT PRESS
Atlanta

Copyright©2018 By Tosha S. Anderson

Published by ANEW POINT PRESS-Atlanta

All rights reserved. No parts of this book may be used or reproduced, stored, or transmitted in any manner whatsoever without written permission from the publisher, except in the case of brief quotations embodied in critical articles and reviews.

All Scripture quotations in this book are taken from the New King James Version & New International Version, Copyright©1979, 1980, 1982 by Thomas Nelson, Publishers. Used by permission.

ISBN 978-1-7342757-0-4

Printed in the United States of America

Contents

Acknowledgments 1

Forward 5

Preface 11

Get Your Mind Right 15

Be Okay with Saying 'No' 55

Taking the plunge 101

Shake Off the Naysayers/Ignore the Haters ... 121

Walk in His Authority 139

Don't Look Back 157

Stay the Course 179

Live in Victory! 195

Acknowledgments

With special thanks:

To my Heavenly Father, for giving me the courage to walk in my purpose, for granting me the drive to not give up on my dream, for giving me the insight to put my thoughts to paper and if I might say wasn't easy at times.

To my husband, Wendell, for his support and encouragement to get it done, for his giving up of our time to allow me time to write.

To my children, for being cool with sharing me with others. For humoring me when I just wanted to be silly.

To my parents, Larry and Clara, for giving me life. For being available when I needed you.

To my siblings, Zorrida and Carlo, for ALWAYS being my cheering squad, for saying yes when I needed your help and believing in me when sometimes I didn't believe in myself.

To my family and friends, Momma Nunn, Carmalita, Margaret, Mary, Sherrie, Erica, Tabitha, and Nadeen for praying for me and ensuring I am covered. For seeing something in me and encouraging me through this process.

Acknowledgements

To Tonya for kick-starting the editing process with me and Morshe, for taking such great care of my baby and helping me through the final editing stage.

To Mary for assisting me with putting my thoughts to paper for the cover and Best Services for taking those ideas and polishing them to perfection.

To Rohit for formatting the heck out of the interior of my book.

Forward

When my wife asked me to write this forward, I was surprised as well as flattered. In order to try and do this to reflect my feelings about my wife, I did a little research. Since being honest was the first thing that stood out to me in writing a forward, I was relieved because that is all I can be when it comes to her.

My wife has always had people reaching out to her since I've known her. Whether they needed her opinion, prayer, or for her to just be present, she made an effort to be there. She was the ear to most of her family and friends.

In each chapter from Get Your Mind Right to Live in Victory, I can attest that my wife lives each one to the fullest of her ability. For her to write this book is just a mirror of how she encourages, mentors, instructs and counsels those she comes in contact with.

My wife desires for you, the reader, to make sure you pay attention to how life issues affect YOU. She encourages us to say NO and be okay with it. She reminds us of who we are and whose we are when we put God first. So, as I stand with my wife and the wonderful job she has done, I want to encourage you to stay the course as you Choose You and Live in Victory!

Wendell

Forward

I love and adore my mother because she is caring and has a selfless heart. If I could describe my mom with one word, it would be...well, that's the thing, there isn't just one word to describe her. I say this because she means too much to me for only one word. So what I will do is provide three words; caring, open-minded, and non-judgmental.

My mom is very comfortable with who she is and has taught me how to embrace who I am. Because she is non-judgmental, I am able to come to her about almost anything. My mom encourages me to ask questions and to stand firm on what I believe. I am so proud of what she has done, not just for us but also for those she comes in contact with.

Noah

My mom is the most loveable and adorable person you could ever meet. She has been the best teacher for us in school and in life. She is the kind of mom that is always there for you no matter what, and she has never given up on us. My mom pushes us to be whoever we want and is there to support us along the way.

She tries to make you laugh even when she is not very funny, BUT you know it comes from her heart, so you just gotta laugh. I am very happy that my mom has accomplished her dream, and I believe that as you read this book you will see her as we do (encourager), and you will enjoy it too.

Zack

Forward

When I think about my mother, Tosha S. Anderson, I think about greatness! I'm my mother's first-born child, and I've watched her do and go through so much. I'm so proud of her and the things she has accomplished. She inspires me in so many ways. I've watched her go from working in a Daycare Center to owning her own, and reading books to kids, to writing her own. Then she graduated from college. I can't recall anyone in my family to do that!

In her life, she decided to make herself a priority and follow her passion, and she encourages each of us to do the same. Now she's counseling and volunteering in the community. Without her prayers and concern for me, I don't know where I would be. I love my mother dearly.

I Choose Me

She is a positive, understanding, loving, and reliable Woman of God. Like glue, she keeps the family and those around her together.

Tre'i

Preface

This book was written to encourage, bring hope, and prayerfully, growth to the reader. The purpose of ***I Choose ME,*** is to assist you the reader, in finding your voice and be true to it. This book is meant to be an easy read, a book that anyone at any age could comprehend and follow, one of those books that feel like you are sharing with a friend or accountability partner.

In life, it's hard sometimes to find time for self. In this book, you will be presented with thought-provoking questions that can aid you in finding your strength to make life's journey all about you.

The world we live in is fast and busy, and if you are not intentional about how you move through it, you will get stuck catering to everyone except you. My desire is to see people FREE and getting there doesn't take complicated terms and numerous steps to achieve it. That freedom allows you to come into the knowledge of your loving Father, who also wants for you that same FREEDOM!

My journey to this freedom has not always been easy. I had to accept the fact that Jehovah loves me unconditionally, which then allowed me to embrace that I too, should love myself the same. This book was written for the sole purpose

Preface

of you to accept Christ's love as truth and to recognize that He knows your worth. What a beautiful thing it would be for you to know it as well. When we finally come into this truth, we have to learn to be a little selfish. Selfish enough to accept you, embrace you and love you at all cost. That means rearranging your priorities so that YOU are #1. Once you can make that connection, **then** you will be able to say, "I Choose ME" and finally take the stand to make it ALL about You!!!

Get Your Mind Right

> " Let this mind be in you, which is also in Christ Jesus: "
>
> Philippians 2:5 (KJV)

The mind is "the complex of elements in an individual that feels, thinks, perceives, wills and reasons. The healthy condition of the mental faculties; intention, desire."(Webster's Seventh New Collegiate Dictionary). When you are approaching a new thing, for it to unveil any sense of success you must ensure that your mind is right. The five senses assist the human brain in the decision-making process. Those things you see and hear can sway you on deciding what you will do in a particular situation. So, how do you know when you are not being led by those senses? When you take the information you know (facts), the information you have heard (hearsay), and remove your personal feelings (emotions), THEN dissect it all to see if it lines up with the word of God for you.

You know that you are moving in the right direction when you have the ability to move about with an "I got this" mindset because you choose to walk in faith and not fear. BOOM! Your mind is most definitely in the right place to make the right decision at that moment. Now, this process is not a one-time action, but it's a daily task.

Because the mind is where all things begin, the enemy will work hard at trying to get and keep you off your game, on a regular basis.

You will not be able to focus or stay focused on the assignment at hand if your mind is constantly wandering. Not to mention the variety of things that the enemy will keep putting before you to add to your day. This will only cause you to feel heavy and frustrated so that starting something new appears to be too much today, tomorrow, or any other day. That is why there are so many books designed to assist you in getting your mind right as you start your day. What you choose to allow to be your focus at the start of your day is crucial because it sets the tone for the remainder of your day.

Are You Starting Strong?

Let's look for a moment at meditation. Meditation is about taking the time to calm and quiet the mind from all the daily clutter and chatter. It's about sitting still to allow yourself time to focus on your breathing, which settles the busyness of your constant thinking, in order for your mind to be cleared. Another thing of importance is eating a balanced breakfast. Now for me, this was hard because I've never been a breakfast person. Seeing that I choose ME, starting my day off with a balanced meal seems to be the best thing to put into practice to ensure my mind is set. To help you create a balanced breakfast, take a look at these suggestions (always listen to your body):

*Apples are a great way to kick start your day, and it has enough natural sugar (13grams) to help you stay awake and alert.

*Eggs are loaded with omega 3's and will keep you full longer as well as keep you charged longer throughout the day.

*Honey makes the body wake up because it takes energy to break it down.

*Oatmeal helps you stay full and boosts your metabolism for the day.

These are just a few options to jump-start your body, as you work on getting your mind right in the pursuit of making it all about you! As you will see along this journey, life is all about choices. Remember what I said about those senses? Pay close attention to what you hear and listen to as you stretch out to begin your day; there is a difference you know. Hearing is all about the sound, while listening is something you choose to do. You have to decide to pay attention to what is being said when you listen; it's a choice. So how about listening to something positive whether it be a song of praise, motivational CD, radio, and even your very own voice to jump-start your morning?

Since I kind of like the sound of my own voice, I enjoy giving myself a pep talk by declaring God's word over my day, my life and everything I set my hands to do. For example: "I can do all things through Christ which strengthens me," "I am fearfully and wonderfully made," "The Lord is my shepherd, and I shall not want," "I am confident, capable and content," "I am worthy of all the best that life has to offer," and "Goodness and mercy shall follow me all the days of my life."

As a believer, I understand what the Word says about who I am and what I'm capable of doing through God BUT, if my mind is not in the right place, I can hear it and even know this information and still think I'm not worthy enough to believe it for ME. It is imperative to be intentional about what you allow to flow through your mind. The scripture states in Philippians 4:8 (KJV), "Finally, brethren, whatsoever things are true, whatsoever things are honest, whatsoever things are just, whatsoever things are pure, whatsoever things are lovely, whatsoever things are of good report; if there be any virtue, and if there be any praise, think on these things." To truly be able to make it all about you, your mind needs to be transformed daily so that you can create the life you deserve.

When you have high levels of self-confidence and are focused on succeeding, your mind will be ready for any challenge that comes your way; because they will. To assist you with this task, consider practicing a few things that have been helpful to me:

*Imagine: envision yourself performing well. Rehearse this positive outcome as needed because it will build self- confidence in your ability to perform your best.

*Self-Talk: allow the conversation to focus on reminding yourself that you are capable of doing the job and doing it well. While speaking to yourself positively, you also dispel negative thoughts of potential failure.

*Meditation: the time you carve out for yourself to tap into that place of peace is essential to how well you perform. Think about the things that relax you. Closing your eyes can be helpful to the process as well as controlling your breathing. Allow each inhalation to bring forth positivity and each exhalation, the release of negativity. Creating opportunities to do these things decrease your anxiety and help you stay in control of your mental state.

Do not allow the enemy to place thoughts into your mind that are contrary to the Word of God. Stop accepting the scraps that he wants to give you and then convince you that it is the best you can do. You deserve the best right now, not in a little while, but you must get it in your head that you deserve it. The Word backs it up, "Beloved, I wish above all things that thou mayest prosper and be in health, even as thy soul prospereth." 3 John 1:2 (KJV). God desires us to be in complete health as we go forth in our purpose for Him, and our mental health is the prime area to start.

Are You Willing To Be Selfish?

Since you have decided to choose YOU, at some point, with this boldness, you will have to be selfish. New Webster's Dictionary defines selfish as "devoted unduly to self; influenced by a view to private advantage." I grew up like most of you, being told to share and don't be selfish, and as I got older, the same was practiced. Keeping what you had, or doing something just for you had a negative connotation associated with it. But for what you desire to accomplish, it's time to get selfish for real, for real. LOL.

Now let me say that I'm not advocating to be disinterested nor unconcerned about the needs of others, especially those in your circle, but I am; however, saying YOU are your first priority (outside of God that is). Due to the fact that I heard those comments over and over for so many years growing up, everyone else was my first priority. I thought taking care of me was taboo.

The few times that I was daring enough to do something for myself, I was left with a feeling of guilt, sometimes by the people in my circle, but most of the time, it was an internal battle. When I think about it now, I shake my head. I was forever allowing myself to put others before me "ALL" the time. Again, as I stated before, there is absolutely nothing wrong with doing for others; after all, it is our mandate as believers, according to Matthew 22:39 (KJV), "thou shalt love thy neighbor as thy self."

Now check this out. How can you love your neighbor as you love yourself if you don't love you OR even know how to love you? Do you even know how to begin to take this journey of giving yourself permission to make it "All About You"?

Get Your Mind Right

How selfish are you really willing to be? My intention is not to offend, step on your toes, or create a barrier between you and those you love. What I do intend, is to assist you in realizing the awesome things you can tap into if you would only be a little selfish. Selfish with your time, selfish with your resources, selfish with your body, and selfish with your heart. You are precious, and all that makes up who you are is precious as well. You can't give your best if you have not had the opportunity to deposit the best. Bottom line, when you take care of you, then and only then can you truly give and be your best for those around you.

So, let's shift the necessary gears, make the needed adjustments, and be 100 percent intentional in ensuring that your mind is in tip-top shape, for where God desires to take you. If you haven't noticed already, you need to be committed to getting your mind right. So, I'll ask you a question...How bad do you want it? You must be at a point of feeling that you are sick and tired of going through the same repetitious cycle over and over and still not getting anywhere.

- Being committed means staying with a thing/routine until it becomes your habit just like breathing.
- Being committed means to stay with something no matter what happens, no matter how difficult things may get, you stay the course day in day out.

- Being committed means staying on the journey regardless of what others may say.

When you are committed, you are focused on the task at hand, and you are not easily distracted. If you are NOT yet committed to your growth, you better forge ahead if you want to see productive progress. If you are not committed to YOU in this process, you better get there fast.

After saying all that, let me take a minute to be transparent. I have struggled with an issue my entire life, and even as I write, I'm still fighting this battle. I have never been diagnosed as obese, but my weight has been an issue for me off and on for many years. For my age and height, I've always been a little over the range to be considered in good shape or healthy, if you will.

Each time I wanted to lose weight, I could never seem to quit eating certain foods, but I was able to set realistic goals and have those good self-talk moments daily to encourage and motivate myself to go for it. Then one day, I took a long look at ME internally and externally, and I didn't like what I saw. I used food as my means of self-medicating when I was hurting, upset, angry, and disappointed. I turned to food to soothe the emotions I experienced, and that was so very unhealthy.

When I came to terms with the fact that I "was" an emotional eater, I felt that I could finally conquer it because I now knew my triggers. I had that "I got this" moment like Rocky during his training phase. My arms were up, and I felt that

I could conquer the world. I was able at that time to shed anywhere from fifteen to twenty pounds and was enjoying the process. It wasn't hard, but you do know that life didn't stop happening just because I wanted to lose weight and get healthy. I had days that were great, and I had days that were an absolute disaster. What I want to say to you is PLEASE, PLEASE, PLEASE, DO NOT GIVE UP! You are human, and it is okay to stumble, heck even fail. God's grace is sufficient for you at this very moment. Now I also don't want you to try and use that as an excuse to intentionally indulge in ANYthing or self-sabotage then say, "God knows my heart" because you best believe, He 'knows' your heart. So let me just say, STOP IT, or should I say DON'T EVEN TRY IT!

Your goal at this point is to have your mind in the right place, and what that says is, if you make an honest mistake, you're strong enough to intentionally get back on track quickly. Why? Because your life depends on it. Take a minute and think about that last statement. Go ahead, really process it because when you come to terms with what that really means, you will never be the same. Just in case you haven't connected the dots: high blood pressure, heart disease, diabetes, anxiety, depression, and obesity just to name a few. Your life really does depend on making these necessary changes.

Once your mind is clear and your focus is set on victory, you have then stepped into a realm of newness. You are no longer the same. There is a fire inside of you that's burning to do something great. When your mind is right, you become fearless, not reckless. Fearless, because all you choose to see is the end result instead of settling on your current state.

Keep in mind that failure should not be in your vocabulary or mindset. Let me clarify this, you will fail, but the thing that separates you from everyone else is your desire to not stay there. What you will not do is stay and take up residence in failure. You will learn from your choices and grow.

Obstacles will come, naysayers will be there, but now you are focused on accomplishing the goal or the assignment given. If you put on your blinders, you will be able to get focused. You know what I mean when I say blinders right? It's the material that is placed on the side of a horse's eyes. Those blinders are put in place to keep the horse set for the journey ahead. The blinders keep the horse from being distracted by all the things around it. So, my plea to you is, put the blinders on, seriously like right NOW!

On this journey of Choosing You, you do not need ANY distractions from anyone because it will only slow you down from getting to your final destination.

- Distractions will cause you to second guess yourself.
- Distractions will cause you to lose focus.
- Distractions will pull you away from what you are supposed to do.

But remember, because your mind is in the right place, you are committed and intentional about you. So, therefore, when the distractions come, because they will, you will not sit there giving attention to them but rather recognize them for what they are, then allow the Father to bring you out of it.

According to I Corinthians 10:13, God will NOT allow you to be tempted beyond your ability, and even in that, He loves you so much that He makes the way of escape for you to endure it. What an awesome God we serve!

Let's look at that word ENDURE. According to the Oxford Dictionary, endure means to "suffer patiently." After looking at that, I thought how or why would you put 'suffer' and 'patiently' together and then place it as a part of our journey? I thought, really GOD! Then I was reminded of the previous scripture I Corinthians 10:13. Right away, my attitude shifted to alright Father; because you have my back, I am reassured that the suffering will not last always. I'll continue on. With this enduring, doors will be closed, and the word NO will be heard.

Are you still willing to stretch yourself past the pain and disappointment to achieve your goal?

So, when life hands you lemons, why not make something different like lemon bars or even try your hand at candied lemon peels because everybody wants to try and make lemonade. LOL. Believe it or not, there is something good about enduring. Enduring will give you strength if you allow it. When unpleasant situations present themselves, and your mind is made up, enduring allows you to gain strength for the next situation. Because you are committed, you stay the course with the intention of getting another step closer to your VICTORY.

If you continue to stay the course, strength will bring its partner boldness, and when they show up, they may surprise even you. Please don't confuse boldness with arrogance because they are

NOT the same. Strength and boldness will rise up in you and kick fears butt because NOW, everything doesn't shake you or make you feel that you are not able to accomplish what you have set out to do. That boldness will give you the confidence to step out and start something new that you would have ordinarily never had the nerve to try.

This brings me back to my struggle with my weight. As I stated before, I visited this place multiple times don't judge. LOL. I remember sitting in my doctor's office wondering how I got to the place of talking about the need to lose weight with my doctor. I've had this conversation with myself many times but now I'm being put in the uncomfortable position of having to discuss that which makes me uneasy with my physician. This makes it really real now. It seemed to have snuck up to bite me on the backside. Driving home, rage rose up in me, because I allowed myself to get to this place. I shifted gears almost immediately and started to organize a strategy so that I could put this mess to rest once and for all.

Once home, I began writing what my plan of action would be, what could I eliminate now, and what I could gradually let go. After I established an outline and purchased the food, I took off with full force. When I started my first week, I realized that the struggle was real. This run out the gate with enthusiasm sounded good, but it was extremely hard this time. I kept restarting and failing. I'd try another alternative and fail again.

I Choose Me

I know I'm not the only person that has been in this position, maybe not with dieting but a struggle is a struggle.

My intentions were great, my motivation was even better, but I finally realized I wasn't in the right position to be successful because at that moment my mind was not right. I hadn't had that conversation with myself yet. That conversation where I remind ME that I am worth the effort to take better care of myself. God desires for me to be in good health and I'm at my best for those around me when I'm at my healthiest state both physically and mentally. During this process, I had to be brutally honest with myself and really look at me. I'm talking about one of those drop-your-robe kind of looks, where there is no camouflage insight. I couldn't hold on to any excuses because all I had was me there in my birthday gear. I wasn't pleased with what I saw because, at that moment, I realized this isn't healthy, and for me, it didn't make me feel attractive. I love who I am; I just didn't like what I was doing to myself. I needed to get to a place that I desired to take care of the precious vessel that my Father entrusted to me. After all, I only have one of them, and it is my responsibility to take care of it and do it well.

In this phase of getting your mind right, it allows you to take in all this truth and be realistic with what to do next. You will learn that taking baby steps is okay. Each step will not be a quick fix. Some steps will be like an onion; you have to remove things one layer at a time slowly and cautiously. You'll need to come to terms with the fact that these steps are a temporary improvement, but if done right, it can be a permanent fixture for your life. This is true whether or not you are working on your attitude, excessive drinking, promiscuity, etc., being in the right frame of mind is essential for your success.

Don't get hyped with the idea of doing something while your mind is all over the place; otherwise, you will be like the hamster on the wheel, going around and around. You are indeed moving but not successfully getting anywhere. Nothing in this situation has been fully accomplished. You have just tired yourself out without any shifting in position occurring, no growth, no strength, and no witness; therefore, nothing has been added to the kingdom. But when you have the ability to think clearly, you gain the "know-how" to step, leap, jump or even hop off that wheel and figure out how to break free. It's always a good thing to have those naked conversations with yourself because it helps you take ownership of your stuff. There is such a peace when you allow yourself to examine every aspect of you and then accept you and all your flaws yet be willing to make the necessary changes to become the best version of you. Even though some of the changes may be difficult, the end result yields such freedom.

There is a point in life when the light bulb will finally come on, and you get it. I mean, you really get it! Everything begins to make sense, and you know what you need to do, and you feel the strength to get it done. You have the mindset of David when he was confident that he could take on Goliath. In I Samuel 17:48, it gives a reference of David's confidence when it states that he "ran" quickly to fight Goliath while it mentions that Goliath "walked" toward David, which to me shows one man willing to fight and the other was ready to fight, do you see the difference? The mind is a powerful thing. It can ***will*** you to not just live but to live with a purpose. Just like David, you need to be fired up about what you are supposed to be doing. It allows you to properly organize, visualize, step out of your comfort zone and be bold. Here, we go back to that daring word "bold." In order to take on your dreams, your passion, life's journey, and God's calling, you must be willing to be bold!

At this point in your journey, I sincerely hope that you have made the choice to choose you. Really think about that as you wind down this section of the book. Keep in mind that this "Choosing You" and "Being Selfish" is really just about getting things done for YOU and allowing you to be at your best. Your possibilities are endless when you have a made-up mind. For me, losing weight became easier when my mind had concluded that it was the best thing to do for ME. Trying to operate at full throttle when your mind is only 40 percent on board is a disaster waiting to happen. This will only lead to constant failure and disappointment.

I asked you before, and I'll ask you again, "How bad do you want it?" The question is not one that is uncommon for someone to ask when you are talking about the desire to start something new. The only time I believe you can truly answer the question is when you are 100 percent invested in YOU, and you believe in YOU. At this point, you can answer by telling them the steps you are willing to take to see your desires come to fruition.

I would be withholding the best stuff from you if I don't let you in on the main ingredient in getting your mind right. Some of you, I'm sure, have already figured it out, but for those still pondering, it's God the Father. When you completely yield yourself to the Father, He will order your steps in every area of your life.

How Does Yielding Work?

When you yield to something, you hold back from what you are doing to give the right of way to something or someone else. The same holds true for the Father. We must give up, let go, surrender everything and allow Him to have the right of way to bring us victory, freedom, and success. Now it goes without saying, all of these positive end results (victory, success, and freedom) do not come without a fight or without sacrifices. And let me also make it clear that some of these things you will go through to gain that victory will not always be with someone else.

Often, it will be an internal battle so pay attention!

The great thing about yielding is, it gives you the opportunity to surrender EVERYTHING to the Father, even those inner demons we battle every day. He is so loving that He will take them without question, and in return, He will give you peace that will allow you to completely rest in Him. The beautiful thing about yielding to the Father is that although it puts you in a place of vulnerability, there is such serenity in it because you know the extent that He went through to show His love toward you. And because He loves you so much; He wants the very best for you. Read John 3:16 as your proof.

Get Your Mind Right

Let me try to just tie it all together for you. When you make the decision to yield to the Father, you are then stepping into a relationship with him, and it's a personal one at that. In this relationship, you must get to know Him in order for that relationship to reap benefits for BOTH parties, right? Okay, now stay with me. As you spend time with the Father, reading His Word, you gain knowledge into who He is, what He needs from you, as well as what He wants to do for you.

Since this is a relationship, He too sees your needs, wants, and desires. The wonderful thing about the Father is, He desires to bless you so your desires can be fulfilled. Part of building that relationship means choosing you sometimes, and that means loving you enough to make the investment in you! Studying His Word, setting aside time to pray, fast, and surround yourself with like-minded people that can pour into you. Remember it's about YOU!

In other words, time with the Father affords you more strength, power, boldness, joy, and my goodness the list goes on and on. When you gain these gifts, it allows you to hear more clearly for His direction; therefore, giving you a mind that is entangled with His Word, which creates an open door for wisdom. When there is constant clutter in your thinking, you are unable to focus, and it is likely that the Father is not in the midst. Yet, when you go before His throne in humility and cast your concern upon Him, He is faithful to give you the wisdom you need to make the necessary decisions just for YOU. Be sure to be still long enough to hear what He has to say. Are you willing to put the time in so that you can see the results you desire, and allow the Father to be glorified while doing it?

Prayer

Heavenly Father,

I come before you humble as I know how, asking that you have your way in my life. I ask that you rescue me from myself and all my ways that are not like you. Touch my mind and bring healing where hurt, doubt, fear, confusion, and negative thinking reside. Give me wisdom to make clear decisions and allow me to think on things that are just, true, lovely, and of good report. I thank you for keeping me in perfect peace when I keep my mind stayed on you. In your son's name I pray this prayer, believing in faith that you will hear and answer me,

Amen, Amen, Amen!

Journal

This is where you take some of that still time and write out how you feel, the questions you have, and allow the Father to heal, mend, and restore your mind.

Journal

Be Okay with Saying 'No'

" But let your communication be, Yea, yea; Nay, nay: For whatsoever is more than these cometh of evil."

Matthew 5:37 (KJV)

Since this journey is All about you, this process of being okay with saying 'no' would be the next great move. Hearing no can be just as hard as saying no. When you hear that the definition of the noun is: "a negative answer or decision," it doesn't exactly put you in the most joyful mindset. Saying *no* to someone is not about being unloving; it is about being true to what works best for you. When others try to invade your time, resources and emotions, you have the right to make the choice that is best for you. In doing that, sometimes, NO will ultimately be your response.

Understand that when you say NO your mind has to be completely on board, otherwise, the receiver of the *no* may try to convince you that your *no* really shouldn't be a 'no' but a 'yes.' Your job is to stay true to you and the growth that you desire and create those necessary boundaries for those around you. You know what I mean, those slick talkers in your life that will drain you of all that you have if you allow them.

Not only will you have to deal with people trying to talk you out of your NO but you also have to deal with the guilt it may leave you with for having to tell them 'no.' At times, the heart and the mind are at battle when some choices have to be made. When you care for someone, and you know you need to tell them no, your emotions sometimes get caught up in the process.

You don't want to offend them or hurt them for that matter, but if you are not careful in sticking firm to your NO, you will find yourself trying to find a way to avoid saying no by maybe indirectly helping. We can be a mess sometimes, can't we? LOL. It is important for you to keep in mind that you were created to serve not to save. When you keep that at the forefront of your thinking it makes it easier to not get caught playing savior to those around you.

The bottom line is, you are not God! It is not your job to be the sole supplier of other's needs. When you step into that role, you make people dependent on you to come to their aid when they should be looking to the Father as their source. As you continue to cast your cares onto the Father, you should also be seeking His direction when it comes to dealing with others. Your job is to live in such a way that draws them to the Father and not to you as their provider.

The question I really want you to ponder on is, would your NO help or hinder them? Be honest with yourself, and lay it all out. You just might be surprised at what you realize. Of course, I'm not saying you shouldn't do for others but what I am saying is set healthy boundaries for when enough is enough and when NO needs to be your definite response. While setting those boundaries, you must be able to not only say 'no,' but mean it as well. You must be able to stand on your NO and be courageous while doing it. Your heart's desire should be to help, not hinder them when you deliver your *no*.

Now if you are anything like I "was," (notice I said was), saying 'no' was especially hard when it came to family. I could have the *no* in my mind and almost ready to roll it off my tongue, but before their spiel on what their need was, I was saying, "let me see what I can do," and you know what, I would try to make it happen. The crazy thing was that in my gut, I knew NO should have been my response. Often, it had nothing to do with whether or not I was able to assist in their need, but it had more to do with if I would be interfering with God's plan.

Then there are the times when I knew the person's reputation, and I still ignored the *no* that was trying to come forth. Once everything settled, I was left upset that I didn't receive what I was promised even though I knew before I interfered that it was going to go down as it did. Absolutely ludicrous, right? But that is what you do when your mind is not rooted and grounded in the Word of God.

If you happen to be an old softy, then you may have to practice saying no. That may sound funny to you or even feel weird once you think about it. If you are not accustomed to saying no, then let's look at this learned behavior. Find the biggest mirror in your home look directly into it and say "NO!" You may giggle at first because it does feel a little silly. This time look into the mirror and think about your time, your resources, and your energy.

How important is all of these to YOU? Think about giving them up for any and everyone at their beck and call. How does that make you feel? Now give me that NO out of your belly! Remember that your time and everything surrounding it is valuable to you, even if no one else thinks so, use it, and give it, wisely. Do this as often as needed, to boost your confidence, and courage in order to be bold enough to actually execute it.

The reason behind the mirror is to allow you the opportunity to see yourself, see your body language, and see your facial expression. Believe it or not, this little warm-up helps you see what others see when you speak to them. It's important that when you give your NO, you want to ensure that you look like you mean it. In other words, you want your body language, tone, and facial expression to convey the same absolute NO that is coming forth from your lips without a doubt.

What I hope you understand, is it's important to be true to yourself and everyone else and not rude, arrogant, or disrespectful in giving your response. Your response is not meant to be one of ill intent. It is about loving yourself enough, to be honest with those around you for the betterment of both parties, because, at the end of the day, when you are at your best, you give of your best. So, the next time you have to deliver a *no* to your bestie, cousin or even your children, get to the nearest mirror to regain your strength so that you can bellow a tasteful, respectful NO!

Is Being Selfish A Part Of Self-Love?

I can remember talking to someone once, and the discussion was about self-love. As we continued the conversation, I said, "Sometimes you just have to be a little selfish when it comes to taking care of you." The look I received was one that indicated that I might have used the wrong word to get my point across. I tried to ensure that what I stated was clear, and indeed **my** opinion;

then I realized it was exactly the word I needed to use. See, so many people have taken the word selfish as a negative act, wherein some instances it is, BUT when it is used with positive intent, the meaning changes. That is why so many people are in a place of feeling burnt out, used, and at a loss for themselves. This happens when you place everyone else on your to-do-list and leave you and your priorities off.

Are You Giving Or Getting?

I see women especially caught up in the 'give and give' lifestyle when they should be in a 'give and get' lifestyle. With the 'give and give' lifestyle, you find yourself giving, giving, and giving to everyone and every situation. They will attach themselves to you and take and take and take just like that of a leech. And just like a leech, they will cling to you so subtly that you are not immediately aware.

Their desperation for help pulls on you and creates a sort of haze if you will. Like the anesthetic, the leech releases, and you become unaware that they are literally sucking the life (not unto death) out of you. Like the leech, some people will fade away and distance themselves from you after they have siphoned ALL they needed from you. But some people ***you*** will have to remove from your life altogether. I'm sure that some may not like the comparison, but with all the similarities, it just seemed fitting.

Before we move any further, we need to look at the 'give and get' lifestyle. When you are in this type of lifestyle, you are in a place of balance. This way of life is healthy for both parties involved. When you have people in your circle that speak into your life and pour into your current and future endeavors, you then are in a position to do the same for others. It brings balance because you can freely give of your time, talents, and resources when you know you, yourself, have a dependable support system available to help you get what you need in return.

In either case, you must be aware of what's going on around you, or else you will look up and find yourself back on that continual hamster wheel, giving, giving, and giving and not willing to speak up and say no. Or maybe not willing to say no to spare someone's feelings while all along, you are suffering. This, I must say, is unproductive, and, dare I say puts you back in the 'give and give' position. This is not where you want to be. Again, in order for you to keep things "all about you," you have to be willing to get what you need, and at times, it will cause you to be a little selfish with your time and resources, and you need to be okay with it.

Let me make something very clear, everyone or everything that seeks your assistance is NOT out to do you harm or drain you of what belongs to you. I'm also not saying that you should disassociate yourself from helping others. Being of service to others and organizations is a great thing, and it makes you feel good in the process. The issue truly comes to play when you take on too much, and you have consumed your day with other people and other things, and you didn't carve any time for yourself.

So then why do you do it? Is it to hear your name called? In other words, is it for some form of notoriety? Is it because you like being in the spotlight? Or is it that you like the feeling of being needed by someone? If you answered 'yes' to any or all these questions, it's okay. It truly is not the end of the world because we all want to feel needed.

If that need begins to take on the form of pride or arrogance, I need you to check that because you are putting yourself before the Father. It is always about the Father, even as you make this journey all about you, make sure your motive remains pure. Look back at your responses again and if at any point your motive does not have Christ at the forefront, check it and get it right.

Having a well-balanced life is what it's all about. Bringing balance means, keeping a record of what you want to do, and need to do, so that you can actually see where you are spending your time, and figuring out if it is productive. It was confirmed that how you spend your time is important when I heard Denzel Washington say to a group of Harvard University graduates, "Because you are doing a lot more, doesn't mean you are getting a lot more done." I totally agree; I would rather take on one task and do it well than take on several projects and none of them gets completed.

Your time and how you spend it should be important to you. Your goal should be (in my opinion) to live your life to the fullest. In other words, live a life that is well spent. A life well spent is not one tied down with running to and fro, from sun up to sun down for someone else then, at the end of the day, you are unhappy and downright miserable. A well-lived life is one that is intentional.

- Intentional about pursuing its passions.
- Intentional about taking great care of self.
- Intentional to serve others.
- Intentional about being bold and daring.

- Intentional about not giving up.
- Intentional about spending time with the Father daily.

Don't forget, life is all about choosing. We have to make choices all day, every day, and being intentional is also a choice.

Is Sacrifice Really Necessary?

Now again, doing for others is well fine and good, but taking care of you is essential. Let me ask you this. Do you think you are worth the sacrifice? The sacrifice of saying no so that you can be refreshed. The sacrifice of declining the invite because it just doesn't fit your journey, the sacrifice to get up early or stay up late to see your dream come to pass, or the sacrifice of not participating in events because your purpose needs tending to. In order to put you first, it will require you to make a conscious effort. On this journey of self-care, be sure you fully understand why you are really saying no. When you are clear on your *no* then the feeling of guilt will no longer target you.

Living your life should be effortless, and there should be freedom in doing it. When you feel the need to perform and please everyone, what you are doing is mismanaging your priorities. Let me explain what I mean. My priorities are God~ Myself~ Husband~ Children (everything else follows).

When I operate in this order, I have complete balance. However, when I choose (for whatever reason) to move out of this divine order, chaos for me is inevitable.

As a Christian, when I don't take time to spend with my Heavenly Father and adhere to His direction, as I said, chaos will follow. That is when I know that I am not living out my best life as a wife, mother or professional. What I have done is allowed my priorities to shift, which causes me to operate in my flesh, and I guarantee you that nobody benefits from that.

Operating in the flesh is a form of reacting (not responding) to your emotions and situations, which can be fickle from one minute to the next. When you move in this manner all day, it's detrimental to everyone around you. On the flip side, when you choose to operate under the guidance of the spirit of God and the enemy begins to stir up his mess, you are more prone to tackle any situation he throws at you with grace. Now, let's just say that your list of priorities may look totally different than mine, and that's okay, just as long as you know what your top priority should be, and you respect it, go ahead and do you.

Let's go back for a moment and further discuss the importance of your *no*. I believe understanding your no helps you in three areas:

1. **Maintain Control:** Since it is your life, who better to be in control of it than you (to the degree that God gives you). You set the tone for your life, destiny, and future. When you maintain control, you teach people how to treat you. Do you see

Be Okay With Saying 'No'

why spending time with 'you' is so important? You can't teach people anything about 'you' if you don't know you. When you make the time for you, you learn the things that make you tick as well as the things that tick you off. You realize your likes and dislikes, your strong areas, and those area's growth and maturity need to hover over. Then and only then can you teach anybody about you or how to treat you for that matter.

When you are in control, no one can tell you what you can and cannot do; that is your job. Nobody can take that control from you unless you give it. So, go defy the odds, break down barriers and even wow yourself. When you maintain control it will exude from every manner of your being, and people will see it and respect it. Now, they still may not like you or even acknowledge what you do, but they can't deny who you are, they see you believe that.

Maintaining control is not about pride, arrogance, or force, it is about setting a standard and living by that standard, so much so, those around you get pulled in and desire to emulate you. This type of control mimics self-confidence, and there's just something sexy about a confident person, well it is. LOL. Maintaining this kind of control allows you to boldly walk in the authority that the Father has given you. This causes opportunities to come chasing you down and not the other way around. When you align those priorities we spoke about, you not only will be able to walk in the authority that the Father has given you, but it will also birth power. Now just think if you will; what type of impact could you have on those around you when you maintain this kind of control?

2. **Know your Limitations:** When you are aware of your strengths and areas of growth, you won't put yourself in anything that doesn't benefit or grow you. I did make it clear that making it all about you will require you to be a bit selfish, so when I say it needs to benefit you, this is also another one of those times that you have to be selfish. In other words, if what someone wants you to do will compromise your integrity, cause you to become stagnant, or hinder/hurt you (physically, mentally, or spiritually) then an assured NO should be your response.

When you know your limitations, you will remain in your lane, and when you are tempted to change lanes, wisdom kicks in and reminds you to return to the lane that best suits you and your situation. Wisdom in this area is very important because it helps you to be okay with your limitations. Being okay with them should not be a form of settling, so don't get too relaxed, but it is to bring awareness and clarity because it is only temporary. Let me quickly say that knowing your limitations is not to say you are incapable of doing a thing, but what it says is that you are wise enough to discern that every investment, every offer, or everything is not meant for you.

Your goal should always be about growth, even in your moments of struggle, for there is a lesson in that too. I like it best when Joel 3:10 (KJV) says, "Let the weak say, I am strong." For me, this is speaking to the end result of your situation. You know what you desire to be/do despite what your current state might be, and you choose to put God's Word in faith over your life and situation. It also doesn't mean, you are to walk around in denial to your reality. What it does say is, when you trust God and His Word enough, then speak it over your life, while believing that His grace is sufficient for you, watch out because He won't withhold no good thing from you!

3. **Remain in your Place:** Your place is not to be god or play god to anyone, yet you have a responsibility to draw them to Him. When you are out of your place, you become their god. They

rely on you to fix their issues, they come to you as their soundboard, and they run to you to get their okay to do what they want to do, that my dear is not your place. When you see that they are trying to move you out of your place, quickly re-route them to the Father. As they commit their situations and circumstances to Him, He will direct them on what to do and who to go to.

When you do this, you are not shutting them out; you are teaching them how to put their trust in the Father, where it should be. The more you remain in your place, the more balanced you become. Keep on the hat that the Father has placed on you for this moment or season. This way people can recognize your role. Too often, we place too much on ourselves out of the fear of saying 'no,' then we are left trying to fix the jacked-up remnants of someone else's mess. Wow, I'm tired just saying it all. Imagine how draining that can be trying to figure all that out. Help when you can, but never be that #1 go-to for anyone. That is and should be the Father's place; I need you to just remain in your place.

Although these points are significant on their own, they really are intertwined. If you allow yourself to be open about your fears, concerns, needs, wants, weaknesses, strengths, passions, joys, dreams, insecurities, and hopes, freedom will take place. A great way to do this is to write it out. Create a list, and for starters, put "Identity Issues" at the top of the paper (the list will vary depending on YOU) then put what the issue is (for example, body image). At this point, you have identified your issue specifically now look at what concerns you have with your body (for example, face fat, stomach huge). Then list how these images make you feel (for example, insecure) and how do you cope with how you feel (for example dress to camouflage my body, desire to eat more).

Once the list is done, it may be painful to look at, take your time, and remember it's all about you. When you are ready to look back at your list, let's add what you can do to change the way you cope and the way you view your issue (for example, create healthy eating habits, speak loving things to yourself). There is a lot of further work that you will have to do to get through some issues you may have, but this is just a very basic start. The bottom line is getting you to a place of loving you right where you are.

Now before we go any further, do you think that I forgot about the importance of saying NO to self? There are times when things come your way that sound good, look good, and may even feel good if you partake in it. What I want you to think about real quick is:

- Will this situation grow you?
- Are there any godly benefits?
- Could it be detrimental to your health?

If you can't say yes to the first two questions and no to the last question then you should be saying NO to yourself (loudly if necessary). On this road to getting healthy, when someone asks if I want something, I have learned to be truthful by saying, "I would really like to have some BUT I do not need it. Thanks." It allows you to be honest with others and yourself. A need and a want are not the same. This journey is not about trampling on people so you can soar, it is about looking at all aspects of your life and dealing with all of it openly and honestly, and that means dealing with YOU!

Saying NO to you requires discipline just as it does with anyone else, and if I may say so, it requires more discipline. When dealing with *you* there is no one to confront you but *you*. You may tend to try and override some stuff, but don't do it because people are watching how you respond. "Let not your good be evil spoken of" (Roman

14:16, KJV). Make sure your expectations of others and your behavior lines up with the will of God. In other words, you shouldn't expect others to treat you with respect and honor, when you don't even respect and honor yourself enough to exercise restraint and say NO.

Don't allow the enemy to place these negative images of what you are not and what you cannot do **now** as truth because God has given you everything you need to be your very best. The enemy does not want you to believe it, so he constantly brings and creates distracting issues to cloud your mind and your viewpoint. I asked you before, and I'll ask you again, are you worth the sacrifice? Because you have to be willing to fight back and gain control of who you are and recognize your limitations so that you can remain in the place to receive what the Father has for you.

Some sacrifices might be to cut up those credit cards, surround yourself with people doing what you desire, getting up early to research, turning down events to do the work, and lots of study in your field of interest. I will be the first to say that it will be scary at times, and you will fail sometimes and want to give up, but don't you dare do it!

There is such peace in knowing and accepting who you are. Because of this peace, you will gain the strength to leap out and begin this new journey of choosing you. So, let me answer the question for you. YES, you are so worth the sacrifice of being intentional to be and do your best for the Father. Do you realize that you were not only chosen but after He chose you He redeemed and forgave you? Sometimes you have to remind yourself of this so that you can dismiss the mess the enemy keeps trying to hang over your head.

While going over your list, you will begin to realize that these feelings of inadequacy are all lies; you are not less than. You are equipped; you are not helpless nor are you alone. When you take your quiet time, don't forget to invite the Father to join you. He is a gentleman, He won't force Himself on you. Allow yourself to bask in His love and watch how easy praying then becomes. Listen, we all have flaws and insecurities, and that is okay, but you cannot sit in those flaws and allow those insecurities to blind you from the truth.

Love and embrace all of you until your change comes. As the renowned speaker, Les Brown says in his motivational speeches, "You have to be hungry" for what you desire to do in life.

How Hungry Are You?

Are you willing to pour into you what is needed to not only receive what you deserve but to also be a blessing to someone else?

- Are you hungry enough to not allow other people's issues to become your issues?
- Are you hungry enough to regain and sustain your peace of mind?

Be Okay With Saying 'No'

When you are hungry, you try to find the very thing that will satisfy the need that lies within. When you begin this search, you start contemplating what do you want, and what do you need right now to fulfill the urge you have? While on this journey, interruptions will come, and if you are hungry, you will ignore them or tell them to hold on a minute, why? Because you're trying to get that need you have met. Doing that takes precedence over everything else right now.

When your hunger has been satisfied, you can then operate at your best for those around you, and most of all, for yourself. This can only take place when you have taken that hunger and made it all about you. You have been given one life and only one body, so why not live it in such a way that shows that you appreciate and cherish the gift as if you know that it is precious.

Let's not forget that we need to not only learn to say 'no' but be okay with saying it as well. Remember what we said earlier? As you commit to your *no*, remember the reason behind the *no*. The *no* does not come from a bad place but a place of self-love. Therefore, when you deliver your 'NO,' do it with love and grace. Now that does not mean you have to offer a full-blown explanation to everyone you deliver a *no* to. You can walk boldly in your 'no' when you know that it's the right thing to do for you.

On this journey, you must maintain your focus and what better way to do that than by beginning your day with affirmations. Let me give you a few things to speak over yourself to kick start your day;

- I am enthusiastic about the success of others as I am about my own.
- I am so strong that nothing can disturb my peace of mind.
- I will give time to the improvement of myself that I have no time to criticize others.
- I think only of the best, to work only for the best, and expect only the best.
- I am too large for worry, too noble for anger, too strong for fear, and too happy to permit the presence of trouble.

When you begin your day, if you set the tone and atmosphere, you can have what you say. You do know that there is power in that which comes forth from your mouth? The scripture puts it this way, "Therefore I say unto you, what things so ever ye desire, when ye pray, believe that ye receive them, and ye shall have them." (Mark 11:24, KJV)

I often tell people to speak the end result, not your current state. In other words, stop talking about what you don't have but believe God for what you have need of. Speak what you desire! When you begin to put your faith in full gear, your NO will become even easier, and when it appears difficult, remember your needs and stick to it.

When people begin to see your consistency, they will either respect it or you can help them come to a place of accepting your decision (now that was nicely said, wasn't it? LOL). For this to successfully work, you must stay in position by making it all about you until you are ready and able to make it all about them. Now that you have gained your momentum and are willing to stick to your guns, understand that you are not alone. You will have days where you are ready and able to give your yea and your nay without conviction. There will also be those times where you will struggle with your love for the person and the desire to do what's best for you.

In those times, again, remind yourself of the commitment you made to YOU. Remind yourself that it's okay to go to the Father for help. Ask yourself, "Will this be a help to my journey or a hindrance?" While weighing out the answer, be honest with yourself and the person you are dealing with. This does not mean that you doing what's best for you, and being honest with the other person, will be pleasing to the hearer, but that is okay too. Once again, you have decided to choose you, and everything and everyone else will follow. What doesn't fall in line was not a blessing nor benefit for your journey, so now your load has gotten a little lighter, all because you stuck to your decision.

My desire for you as you continue on this journey is complete FREEDOM, but as you know, it's all up to you. You have to walk this out on your own, not all alone. When you find yourself in need of wisdom, ask the Father, and He will gladly give it, to assist you in your decision making especially when it comes to saying NO. Think about it, if you are not making wise decisions, you are making foolish ones. LOL. What do you do when that happens? You should take a moment to see what you can learn from it. There is always a lesson in a mess. Once you can recognize it, you won't be so quick to repeat it. My prayer for you is that your eyes be open so that you can clearly see the consequences of your decisions.

When your priorities are in place, you will be in tune with the Father, and there is such strength in that. And of course, confidence drapes on your strength like a well-fitted suit. As I said before, there is nothing like a person walking with confidence. That type of confidence shows those around you that you have integrity. Integrity shows that you love yourself enough to put you as a top priority in your life.

I know for some, this type of selfishness is still frowned upon, but thankfully you have learned better. I give you permission to be positively selfish for the betterment of your life, health, and strength. I am very hopeful that you have gained the courage to begin making life more about you. Be careful to sift through all the tasks, assignments, and requests to determine if it will take you away from your passion/purpose, or will it take you to your purpose/passion. And when all else fails, get back in front of that mirror, I'm just saying. Get ready to invest in YOU because a change is about to come.

Most people don't like change, but you and I know that it is inevitable. This would be a great time to yell, 'NO!!!' Not just because I asked, but because you are now completely free to live "your" life to the fullest without fear or regret. You will be so much better because of it, and if truth be told, those around you will be better for it as well. Don't allow life circumstances to steal your thunder. I'm so excited for you and all the great things the Father has ready for you; you truly are an overcomer! Now let's get out there and live the heck out of your life!

Prayer

Heavenly Father,

I thank you for loving me and teaching me to love myself. I thank you Father, for giving me strength and wisdom to say, 'NO.' Enable me Father, to speak with confidence and love. Help me to also seek you first before I move. Keep your hand of protection over me, as I stand firm in my convictions. Help me, Father, to maintain my identity in you as I serve others. It's in Jesus' name I pray this prayer in faith,

Amen, Amen, Amen!

Journal

This is where you take some of that still time and write out how you feel, the questions you have, and allow the Father to heal, mend, and restore your mind.

Journal

Taking the plunge

" And Peter answered him and said, Lord, if it be thou, bid me come unto thee on the water. And he said, Come. And when Peter was come down out of the ship, he walked on the water, to go to Jesus."

Matthew 14:28-29 (KJV)

When you think about taking the plunge to make it all about you, there is one thing that comes to mind for me, and that is faith. The New Webster Dictionary states faith is complete trust or confidence in something or someone. To take this plunge, you will need to have your faith activated because you are about to step into unknown territory. You can trust in the Father and know that He has your best interests at hand when your faith is activated. Now, you are aware that He won't just leave you hanging all alone because if He brings you to a thing, He will assuredly bring you through it, so take the plunge!

Stay focused now because you are stepping out and investing in you. Be aware that everyone will not be happy about this change. Of course, everyone is ecstatic when you are doing or investing in them, but when you begin to decline events to invest in you, it will be frowned upon by some. Be okay if you start getting the cold shoulder even from your family. Love them regardless, but love you more.

Investing in you is a great thing, and it doesn't have to be a huge production. If you know you need to spruce up your wardrobe, what are you waiting for? Go get your shopping on. Now you aren't trying to break the bank or put your account in the red but feel free to add a few items to your closet. I'm sure you've heard the old adage, "when you look good, you feel good." There are many benefits to investing in you such as increased self-esteem, sharpened awareness, and a strong work ethic. When you say 'no' to others and 'yes' to yourself you are signifying that you are important and you are worth the effort.

So, what are some ways you can invest in you, you might ask? Take a class (educational or just for fun), take better care of your body (exercise, eat healthily), or pursue your passion (work toward your dreams, desires). This is the perfect opportunity to grow your God-given talents, as we've been saying all along. When you are at your best, you give your best. And to be your best, you must be willing to take the plunge and invest in YOU, in other words, be a little selfish and do you.

The first initial transition to saying NO to others may come with a bit of resistance, but again, that's alright. Don't forget; it's all about you. Once you take this plunge and get over the shock that you really took this leap, your energy level will go through the roof. Let me put in this disclaimer, "taking this plunge may not always be a success story." But by no means are you to let this deter you from the process.

Allow your every attempt to become the thread to getting another step closer to your dream. Learn from it, grow from it, but more than anything, do not allow the fumbles to make you give up or become bitter. Remember, it's a good thing to invest in you, even if you have to begin again. Keep in mind the pull you've been feeling is what gave you the strength to actually take the plunge in the first place.

How Should You Handle Fear?

When you begin this journey, fear will assuredly rise up. Fear will tell you that you cannot afford to invest in you, or now is not the right time to choose you. Fear will tell you it won't make a difference or why bother because you won't stick with it. What you have to remember about fear is that it is an untruth emotion. It appears to be real, but in reality, it is full of deceit.

Fear will cause you to become out of balance, which will eventually cripple you from taking the plunge. Love you enough to invest in you no matter where the area of need may be. Now, remember, fear desires to paralyze you, to stop you from loving on you. As I stated early on, faith is essential for you to be able to move past what you see and know and still take the plunge.

Let's look at both faith and fear. Faith says, "I trust beyond what I see," while Fear says, "The unknown will always harm you." Faith says, "I believe even when everything around me urges me to run." Fear says, "You better run." So, I will ask you this, whose report will you believe? According to the Word, God doesn't give us a spirit of fear, so if He didn't give it to you, why are you holding on to it?

Make it all about you and LET IT GO! Don't allow life to roll by, and you not be a part of it, live life to the fullest. Take the time now to enjoy what life has to offer. Repeat after me, "No regrets!" There you go, now go do something spectacular, all just for YOU! Now, before you even say that you don't know if you can do it, letting go, enjoying life, or taking the plunge, ask yourself, "What if I CAN?" Do you want to allow a lie to cripple you on this journey? Don't entertain the mess that the enemy tries to smother you with concerning your abilities, your physical appearance or even your relationships.

The enemy desires to keep you intimidated so that you won't fully recognize your power, which the Father has freely given you. Because He knows that if you acknowledge the existence of this power and authority, making it all about you as well as taking the plunge will be inevitable. Think about it for a moment, if you invest in you then pour into others, and they invest more in themselves, then they pour into someone else; this would be a much more beautiful world.

Let me say that I'm aware that you don't live in a perfect world, and while you can't force nor change anyone else, you can, however, work on you. Don't allow this opportunity to pass you by while wallowing in the lies of the enemy, get back into the mirror and recognize the warrior looking back at you. Speak the Word of God over your fears, brace yourself for the leap and just do it! Remember, when speaking the Word over your fears and emotions, make sure you include Isaiah 41:10 and Philippians 4:6-7 because there is power in the Word of God, and it soothes every worry, doubt, fear and all anxiety you battle on a daily basis.

Before you move any further, let's be very clear on the fact that there are crazy things going on around you, and it can cause you to feel angry, frustrated, and stressed, if and only if you choose to allow it to consume you. But if you desire to make it all about you, your faith will be activated, and you will be able to put fear and every other negative thought captive. You have what it takes to take the plunge. Only you can determine what you are taking the leap into and why. You set the tone for this journey; as the song says, "It's your thang; do what you want to do."

How Strong Is Your Mind?

There's one thing that is needed to make taking the plunge a lot easier, even before faith kicks in, and that's having a made-up mind. As mentioned in chapter one, everything begins in the mind. When you are focused and have a complete understanding of what you want to do, and you understand the importance of you doing it, then taking the plunge will become a great deal easier.

When your mind is clear, your body will follow. When your mind is clear your perspective is sharp and on point. And when you really think about it, having a clear, focused mindset causes you to have clarity in your decision making, it causes you to see things for what they really are. As things are lined up with your mind and way of thinking, taking the plunge on your dreams, desires and passions shifts from scary to exciting.

Since we've been talking about taking the plunge, some may be asking, what is the plunge for? It's the desire you have down in your gut to do a thing, but obstacles keep coming up to distract you from making the necessary moves and some of those obstacles YOU yourself created.

Now, if you take a made-up mind and go forth and pursue your desire no matter how scary it can be, your mindset will begin screaming DO IT! DO IT! DO IT! The plunge comes into play when the research has been done, the forms have been collected then completed and now the final step is to just go for it! "Do what," you still may be asking; Sale your product, offer your services, publish that book, promote that idea or even

Taking The Plunge

volunteer your time. Whatever the plunge is for, DO IT! Do it by Faith no matter the outcome.

Now let's look at another type of plunge, the investing in YOU plunge. If you are that person that does for everyone else, it is high time you take the plunge in doing for "you." After all, you are reading a book titled, "I Choose Me." If you are honest with yourself, you know that you have been neglecting yourself, you have laid aside your needs and wants far too long.

But now is the time to look "you" in the mirror and meet the needs of the person you see in that very mirror. For some people, this may pose a challenge because you have never allowed yourself to be a priority; therefore, you don't know what you need let alone what you might like. Neglect, as you know it, is about to change. For starters, think about what brings you joy, the things that give you peace. Notice, I didn't say the things that make you happy; that's because, for me, happiness has conditions connected to them. Hear me when I say, when the right things are in place, one can then maybe say they are happy, BUT when those things change, what happens to their happiness?

Whereas, joy is constant because you know who you are and in who you belong; therefore, you have everlasting joy no matter what goes on in life, and you can always pull from within to rekindle that God-given gift. Trying to pursue happiness often leads to the very opposite, what a bummer.

Taking The Plunge

But again, this may be a fresh start for some. Once you get the taste of making You a priority, you won't turn back. To pull this off, you know, taking the plunge, do not forget you must be in a good headspace. If not, fear, doubt, and the unknown will say, "Don't even think about it." If you listen to it long enough, you will let the naysayers and your negative self-talk cause you to back up and sit down on your dreams. And you know that not much can be done resting on your laurels. So, don't you dare sit down on your dreams. Go ahead and take the plunge.

As you continue to love on yourself, be encouraged to know that the Father has your back, and He has your best interest at heart. So, after you have done all you know to do, take a deep breath and take the plunge. In other words, step out of your comfort zone. Don't allow your lack to stop you from moving forward, because that is when God will step in and supply that which you have need of. Remember, taking this plunge is about making a move that may be unfamiliar and doing it anyway for the betterment of you and those around you.

By all means, if you have to take a minute to psych yourself up before you take the plunge, that's okay; go ahead. I'll give you that minute. Now don't take too long because someone is waiting for your dreams to be manifested. Your desires, dreams, and passion will be the very thing to help someone along their journey.

Taking The Plunge

So you ready? Okay, here we go, **1.2.3**

JUMP!

Prayer

Heavenly Father,

I thank you for strengthening my mind. I thank you for granting me boldness, filling me with power, and gifting me with the authority to step up and fulfill the desires of my heart. Lord, help me not waiver as I step out on Faith, but continue to be by my side as I take the plunge for you, myself, and for those I serve. It's in Jesus' name I pray this prayer in Faith,

Amen, Amen, Amen!

Journal

This is where you take some of that still time and write out how you feel, the questions you have, and allow the Father to heal, mend, and restore your mind.

Journal

Shake Off the Naysayers/Ignore the Haters

> " If the world hates you, keep in mind that it hated me first."
>
> John 15:18 (NIV)

On this journey of getting to know and understand you, you will encounter people of all kinds. The two you need to watch out for are the Haters and the Naysayers. Brace yourself for the haters, the people that refuse to be happy for another person's success. You know, that person that appears to be on your team, but during every conversation, they can tell you why something won't work or better yet, the person that scrunch up their face in disgust when you begin doing things differently, even when it's for your betterment. Then they will say to you, "So now you too good for..."

Now, don't you dare forget about the Naysayers. Naysayers are those that no matter what is going on, they are ready to engage in excessive complaining. They are the folks that always bring out the worst in the situation and are willing to whine for hours about the most insignificant inconveniences. If you are not careful, they will try and encourage you to employ their mindset.

Can You Be Faithful In Chaos?

When I thought about this chapter, I thought about Joseph, the son of Jacob. So, let's look at Joseph and the Naysayers and Haters that he encountered. The Bible speaks of Joseph (beginning in Genesis 37) as one who was deeply loved by his father, so much so that his father had a multicolored coat made just for him. Joseph faced looks and negative comments daily. In other words, Joseph had haters at a very early age (verse 4). As the story continues, Joseph's brothers became so jealous of the love that his father had for him that they allowed hate to consume their hearts for their very own brother.

Can you imagine what Joseph went through in a house where his brothers hated him and treated him badly day in and day out? Some may say that maybe if Joseph wasn't a tattletale and wasn't always talking about those darn dreams, just maybe his brothers would have treated him differently. But to Joseph's defense, he could only be who God created him to be.

You are like Joseph. God has placed something inside of you, and when you begin to tap into it, outcomes your haters. If you notice in your reading of Joseph, the more he talked about his dreams, the more he was hated, and his Naysayers talked against him. Even the man (his father) who loved him dearly became upset with him to the point that he rebuked (chastise or criticized) Joseph. But in the midst of his rebuke, he kept what Joseph said in consideration. Could it have been because of the call that God placed on Joseph's life?

Think about it like this; when you have been called to do an assignment, you will stand out to those around you no matter what is going on. You may not be trying to bring notice to yourself, but the call undeniably stands out. The anointing creates an aura about you that makes what you say, the way you look, and what you do have purpose and meaning.

That is why, as crazy as Joseph's dream seemed to his father Jacob, he still couldn't help but ponder on Joseph's interpretation. See, as much as your haters speak and your naysayers walk around with a doom and gloom countenance about everything you're doing, they know that you have a call on your life. They know there is something different about you. But because of their own issues and insecurities, they would much rather shine the light on you than welcome the spotlight on themselves.

In the case of Joseph, his brothers hated him so much; they plotted to kill him. Truth be told, it wasn't about Joseph but about the relationship he had with their father. Which confirms James 3:16(NIV), "For where you have envy and selfish ambition, there you find disorder and every evil practice." Brace yourself as Joseph did, because hardship is a part of life's journey and like Joseph, you must have the right perspective as you allow the Father to guide you in every situation. Basically, your haters will try to get you out of the picture and destroy your reputation with the main goal in mind, keeping those around you at a distance, so they are unable to reap from the gifts and talents given to YOU by the Father.

As Joseph had to keep the faith on his journey, you too will need to exercise your faith in God, to be able to operate in love as Joseph did with his brothers. So don't be alarmed if you find your haters and naysayers to be those in your inner circle. Stay true to what you know God has called you to do, LOVE! During this process, you will learn how strong you really are. It takes strength to go past the negative comments and destructive accusations around you. It will take discipline to stay the course. Remember, if He brings you to a thing, He will most definitely bring you through it as well.

Now the naysayers will try to have you in a negative state of mind, to feel that nothing will get better, and you can't do anything with the dream you have inside. The naysayer's job is to get you to lose all hope in what you know in your heart God has given you. If you continue to entertain naysayers, they will kill your dream, even your desire to pursue your dream, "if" you allow them. So, shake off the naysayers, don't allow their drama to become yours. The way to do this is to love "YOU." Life has its own share of issues just for you, so why would you want to add to it by accepting something that rightfully belongs to someone else?   Absolutely accept how God created you.

- Love you enough to reject that mess.
- Love you so much that it becomes sickening to everyone else.
- Love you as He loves you, with all your flaws included.
- Love you enough to want the best for yourself as Christ does. "Beloved, I wish above all things that thou mayest prosper and be in health, even as thy soul prospereth." 3 John 1:2 (KJV).

Let me forewarn you now. When you walk around with your head held high because you finally are at peace with who you are, and you love every aspect of it, the haters will be in an uproar.

I Choose Me

Are you ready for this? Sure you are! You are walking in your purpose child, and if I might say so, you are looking darn good in it. As you begin to walk in this new confidence, the looks and comments will start pouring in. From the hater's standpoint, you think you know it all, cocky and at times appear to be arrogant. When you walk in that boldness and in that reassurance, those around you may not like it or understand it, not because of what you bring to the table (most times) but often because they, themselves, are not there yet.

The key thing is for YOU to stay focused because when you know who you are, you walk in confidence, not arrogance. The confidence is not that you know it all but that you have a relationship with the one who does. See, they have not yet tapped into the love of the Father, nor have they come to the knowledge of His purpose for their life.

Another thing, when you are crippled with fear (most haters are) of the unknown, and you see others walking with assuredness, it can make you bitter and create the attitude of a hater. Don't allow yourself to be distracted by the hater, keep in mind the ball is in your court, and a matter of fact, it has always been there. So how do you want to play this? Because you realize that you don't have to accept the things the enemy wants to give you, right? Recognize that **you are good enough**, and the world's view of you is just that, the world's view.

Keep your eyes on the prize. The prize is YOU and how God desires to use you. When you shake off the naysayers and ignore the haters, you recognize that the call on your life is far more important than the opinion of others. Try taking on the attitude of Joseph...Faithful.

- Faithful to the Lord.
- Faithful to His Word.
- Faithful to the call He has on your life.

I do think it is important to shine the light on a fact that you may not have thought about. You yourself can be the naysayer or hater in your very own journey.

Seriously, think about it; if everyone around you seems to be moving forward and advancing, you can begin to feel stagnant, then you will begin to compare yourself to others. Before long, you start speaking negatively about your abilities, constantly complaining about your circumstances, second-guessing everything you attempt to do, and disgusted about your physical appearance. You know the list can go on and on.

Where Are You Going?

If your mind is not grounded on the Word of God, you can easily have the attitude that nothing is going right, and they never will. This kind of thinking will take you straight to naysayer's lane. When you are not able to celebrate someone else's accomplishments or are always having to say or think something negative about someone else, this can take you tumbling down haters hill.

I Choose Me

Since you have chosen to make this journey all about you, negativity doesn't get a seat, especially a front-row seat in any aspect of your life.

Your primary objective is to grow you, and anything that takes away from that process needs to be removed, ignored, plucked out, and shaken off for your betterment. If it doesn't grow you, it has the potential to harm you. On this journey, you will have to work hard, and that will require strength and wisdom, allow the Father to saturate you with both. You don't want to find yourself entertaining anything that will slow you down on your dream being manifested. You've got work to do. Are you up for the challenge?

Prayer

Heavenly Father,

I thank you for granting me wisdom. Wisdom to recognize and reject all lies of the enemy.

Wisdom to not entertain trickery, false accusations, or even fear. I pray Father, that you will guide me in all truth and allow me to be one who walks in integrity and adheres to the Spirit of truth. It's in Jesus' name I pray this prayer in Faith,

Amen, Amen, Amen!

Journal

This is where you take some of that still time and write out how you feel, the questions you have, and allow the Father to heal, mend, and restore your mind.

Journal

Walk in His Authority

" I have given you authority to trample on snakes and scorpions and to overcome all the power of the enemy; nothing will harm you."

Luke 10:19 (NIV)

I am so excited that you have made it to this chapter. When you think about walking in His authority, what comes to mind? While you are thinking, let me tell you what the word authority means: Authority is defined as the power to give orders, and enforce obedience (Oxford Dictionary). When you consider the definition of Authority and the above scripture, does it make you want to find someone to give an order to? Before you go all Commando, you may want to ensure that you are in a position to give out the order. Well, actually any order for that matter. What do you think you need to have in order to move in any form of authority? If you said power, you are so right, but before you even look at power let's take a quick peek at what you need to have established before power can even fall in place.

Look at it this way, the power needed to walk in authority comes from God. Before He can give (power) of Himself, can He trust you with it? Can He trust you with what is precious to Him? See, this type of giving and receiving is about being in a relationship. When someone is in a relationship, they are able to give freely of themselves. So let me now set the scene for you to understand the need for a relationship with the Father. God loves you so much. He gave His one and only son for the sins of this world, so that YOU can have an opportunity to receive His love fully and not perish in your sin but instead receive everlasting life John 3:16.

The awesome thing about it all is, He just doesn't want you to experience life but that you may have life more abundantly, full of passion and purpose John 10:10. Now when God sent His Son, it wasn't to condemn you because He is aware that 'All' have sinned, and because you are human, you will continue to sin. It's the wonderful gift of His grace that He extends to His children that allows you to be received back unto Him.

It's the sin that separates you from the Father, and you must be willing to take ownership of it to have a relationship with God. Even though God gave His Son for you and me, Christ had a choice in the matter. This shines the light on the question asked earlier, "Can He trust you?" Because it was clear that Christ trusted God so much so that He allowed death to have its way for the sins of someone else (you and me). But the wonderful thing is that He rose with All Power, and He was able to do this because;

- He was in a relationship with the Father.
- He proved that He could be trusted.

- He showed that He Himself trusted.

If you want to be in a relationship with the Father, now is a perfect time. So let's say this simple prayer and become a part of the body of Christ,

Dear God, I know I'm a sinner, and I ask for your forgiveness. I believe Jesus Christ is your son. I believe that He died for my sins and that you raised Him to life. I want to trust Him as my Savior and follow Him as Lord, from this day forward. Guide my life and help me to do your will, I pray this in the name of Jesus. Amen.

If you took the time to accept Christ and surrendered your life to God, then my dear, WELCOME, WELCOME!!! It is indeed a privilege to walk this out with family. As you find your way around this new commitment, let me just say it's like any other relationship in some respect. You must be intentional in getting to know the Father. The way to do this is to spend time with Him, study His Word, worship, and pray. In other words, court Him. The more time you spend with Him, the more you understand Him. It doesn't end at accepting Him, there's work that needs to be done. Again, someone is waiting for what you have.

Seek to do things that please Him, that is what you do when you are in a committed relationship. When you are in a relationship, you are willing to give up your right for someone else's wrong. With this kind of relationship, you know without question that He has your back. The more you become open to where God is trying to take the relationship, the more His power becomes evident.

Relax in what He wants to do through you on this journey; it will build your faith and trust in what He is able to do. During this time, make sure you keep the lines of communication wide open. Obstacles will arise, but you will need to pull on and rely on that line to receive the help you need. This courtship period brings about growth and maturity, because of the experiences you have encountered with the Father, has begun taking shape. So, if you are asking, "When does the power come in play?" It is when you have been intentional about spending time with the

Father and studying His Word. Remember the courtship, stay with me now.

So, when you speak a thing, you give it power because of the faith and trust you have in the one who gives it. You do know that life and death are in the power of your tongue, right? Proverb 18:21. But let me throw in this disclaimer: what you speak only has power when you do not doubt but believe and have confidence in the Father. This beautiful gift that God gives should not be displayed as arrogance yet used to uplift, motivate, and even battle for the very life of the body of Christ.

Let me ask you, at this moment in your life, knowing what you know now, are you operating in your God-given power? If not, why? If you have to take a moment to remind yourself of who God is or how much He loves you, do that because we all have those times when we have to encourage, motivate, and remind ourselves of the goodness of the Father so that we can move forward in His will.

Don't allow the enemy to make you feel unworthy, incapable, or weak because there is such greatness in you. The enemy knows this, and he will fight you tooth and nail to have you not operate in it. As a matter of fact, that is why he fights you so hard because he knows the gifts and talents that rest in you. You just need to recognize it and believe it. When you come to the realization of how awesome "YOU" are in Christ, it makes operating in the power of God and the ability to walk in His authority so much easier.

Do You Need To Elevate Your Vision?

Try seeing yourself the way your Heavenly Father sees you. He looks at you, and He sees you beyond your past.

- Past your brokenness.
- Past your financial status.
- Past your relationship.
- Past your fear.

He still loves you and desires to use you. It's time you start seeing yourself past your imperfections and focus on what you are capable of doing through Christ, all things great and small. Now, with all this brewing during the courtship, be sure to keep a positive mindset, especially concerning yourself. Think about it like this, how can you command or do anything if you don't have confidence in the fact that you can or that you are qualified to do it, as well as not having the faith in the one that qualified you? This type of lack will have those around you feeling the same doubt that you feel, which does not work when you are striving to walk in His authority.

Let's do a quick recap before we are fully able to understand the importance of the authority.

- First, you must be in a relationship with the Father to receive the ability to walk in authority.
- Second, in order to activate the power that accompanies the authority, you must

believe in yourself and the gifts that God placed in you Ephesians 2:8-9.

- Lastly, in order to walk in the boldness of authority, you need to pull on the faith that resides within you because without it, it's impossible to please Him Hebrew 11:6.

When you begin to walk in authority, keep in mind that it is not in your strength that you will be able to pull anything off, it's the strength from the Father. There are times you will feel inadequate to give out instructions or take the lead in any area. This is when you have to pull on your faith to encourage yourself to look past what you feel and past what you do not see and move anyway.

Walking in authority says you can move in areas where your education or title won't allow you because you have that awesome relationship with the Father, and the power of the Holy Spirit is operating. You can now tap into the unconditional love the Father has for you and believe you truly can do all things through Him. This way of thinking fuels the spirit within and stirs up the gifts in you. The anointed boldness will come over you, and you will feel as if you can conquer anything, NOT because you are all that, but because you know who resides on the inside of you.

When you get to that place of unwavering faith (Hebrew 11:1), you are able to walk in "His" authority. Walking in this kind of authority causes things to be moved, changed, healed, and restored. Are you ready for this type of authority?

Prayer

Heavenly Father,

I pray that you would give me a heart that is quick to confess my mistakes and renew a steadfast spirit in me. As I desire to walk in your authority, place a hedge of protection around me. Help me to see myself the way you do. Fill me with your power and grant me wisdom to operate in your divine will. Help me to stay humble as I walk with boldness to fulfill the assignment that you have placed in my life. In Jesus' name, I pray,

Amen, Amen, Amen!

Journal

This is where you take some of that still time and write out how you feel, the questions you have, and allow the Father to heal, mend, and restore your mind.

Journal

Don't Look Back

" Therefore, if anyone is in Christ, the new creation has come: The old has gone, the new is here!"

II Corinthians 5:17 (NIV)

On this journey called life, I believe you get to a place that you feel something is missing or that there has to be more in life than the current state you are in. When you have an open mind and heart, you will feel the tug of God for your life. That feeling of something missing nags on your spirit until it is fulfilled. Often, you will find yourself filling it with sex, alcohol, food, shopping, work, activities, etc. thinking it will calm that gut-wrenching emptiness you feel. Then you stand back to take inventory of your life, your day, and you find it FULL, actually maxed out, but that feeling is still there with a pulse of its own. That tug you feel is the gentle love of God, calling you into his precious arms.

At this point, you are still courting Him and you aren't familiar with His voice. So you continue this journey still trying to fill that void. But Psalms 46:1 (NIV) states, "God is our refuge and strength, a very present help in trouble." See, your misappropriating things in the space that God desires to fill is how you can find yourself in trouble.

Once you are able to truly hear God, whether through a friend, co-worker, Pastor/Clergy, or family, "then" you will be able to accept Him as your refuge and strength. That strength will allow you to maintain as He begins to fill you, causing the distractions to be forced out. As you read previously, your commitment to the Father will cause you to spend time with Him, therefore, granting you more strength, wisdom, and boldness which makes the remaining of Psalm 46:2-11 (NIV) attainable, "Therefore we will not fear, even though the earth be removed and though the mountains be carried into the midst of the sea; Though it's waters roar and be troubled, though the mountains shake with its swelling. There is a river whose streams shall make glad the city of God, the holy place of the tabernacle of the Most High. God is in the midst of her, she shall not be moved; God shall help her, just at the break of dawn. The nations raged, the kingdoms were moved; He uttered His voice, the earth melted. The Lord of hosts is with us; the God of Jacob is our refuge. Selah Come, behold the works of the Lord, who has made desolations in the earth. He makes wars cease to the end of the earth; He breaks the bow and cuts the spear in two; He burns the chariot in the fire. Be still and know that I am God; I will be exalted among the nations, I will be exalted in the earth! The Lord of host is with us; the God of Jacob is our refuge. Selah"

As you reflect on what you just read from Psalms 46:2-11, be encouraged in the fact that God desires to be your all in all in EVERY situation life brings your way. When you allow Him into your life completely, He provides you with what you need to walk in boldness, not fear, and to have joy instead of sadness because He is always in the midst of your situation.

What Happens When You Are Still?

You can rest in knowing that He will never leave you nor forsake you even when your battle is within, just be still. Now being still doesn't mean you are confined from doing anything, but I believe it's the opportunity to surrender and recognize YOUR position, and it's many limits, but most of all, become aware of the position of

God in your life. After all, He is Jehovah Jireh, your provider.

Let me also throw out that as you allow the Father to fill you, the sex, food, and shopping may not just leave nicely. You may have to battle a little with those things, and that's okay because the Father is so patient and kind. He will help you during your battle and cause you to know him in the beauty of His Holiness. What a magnificent position to be in. Are you aware of the things **you** have put in place of God? Are you ready to let go of your past? Are you ready to let go and not look back? If not, what's the hold-up?

I really want you to think about these things and be honest with yourself. For example, if you are in a relationship and that relationship consumes your time, energy, and resources. You also find yourself constantly catering to the needs of that relationship. Before long, you realize you haven't spent time studying your Word, haven't been going to church, or even prayed daily. You have now placed that relationship before God. Don't forget, if it does not grow you on your life's journey and it does not reflect the righteousness of God, then you need to re-evaluate that relationship. Notice I said re-evaluate not leave. Don't underestimate the power of prayer. And let me also say, I don't condone domestic violence, so if you are in imminent danger, please seek help immediately.

Anytime you remove yourself from that which has become familiar can be challenging because you have invested time, resources and yourself in it. Change can be hard, even when the situation is destructive, and you know that your ability to leave will prove to be better. So I ask you again, are you ready to let go and not look back? You can do this because God has your back, and if you continue to do what God has given you, you will assuredly reap the benefits in due season Galatians 6:9.

The thing that is important in all of this, and it stands repeating, it's a made-up mind. One that is sick and tired of being sick and tired of your current state. One that is willing to move even though the specifics are not clear. You get to this point when you surrender your fears, concerns, and doubts to the Father and ask him to wash away every negative thought and feeling and give you a sound mind. A mind so sound that standing on his word is automatic. A mind so sound that faith has permanent root in your soul. When your mind is stable and focused, it puts you in a position to stand steady when temptation comes to draw you back to the very thing that you are turning away from. Yes, I did say 'when' temptation comes not 'IF' because you and I know that it is a constant.

You have to be careful in your confession of faith that you don't fall in love with your past and begin to look back at it like Lots wife Gen 19:17-26 (KJV). She was told to leave Sodom, to be exact, "Escape for thy life; look not behind thee, neither stay thou in all the plain; escape to the mountain, lest thou be consumed."

The same warning the Angels gave Lot and his family is the same warning you and I get. You then have to choose will you go or will you stay? When you finally decide to go, you need not look back. Remind yourself that what you have left behind isn't yours anymore because you have chosen to follow the direction of Christ. To successfully make this happen, you have to walk in faith, without hesitation. Again don't look back, turn back, or even linger on the things of your past.

You may be thinking, what's wrong with looking back, taking a peek, or just a short glance at your past? Looking back when God is trying to move you forward displays a lack of trust. When God is doing a thing in you, and you commit to the process, it says that you take the Father at His Word.

Be careful not to become distracted by the noise of your past, nor allow those familiar sounds and smells to try and lure you to look back. That backward glance causes you to lust for the very thing that is unhealthy for you. Looking back says you are not focused on God. This brings me to the parable of a disciple of Jesus, Peter. In the book of Matthew 14:25, the disciples were sent ahead while He took time to pray, then He appeared before them walking on water. Immediately, they became frightened, sounds familiar, doesn't it? Does it kind of remind you of yourself when circumstances are somewhat unclear? But then Peter decided he needed to verify the authenticity of what he thought he saw. So Peter asked, "Lord, if it is you, command me to come to you on the water" v.28.

Do you think Peter really understood the magnitude of his comment? Think about it, that comment requires Peter to step out literally on faith, the same way you are required to do. Once Jesus said, "Come!" he began to walk in obedience toward Jesus, not just because he was focused on Jesus and the directions He gave, but also because if Jesus said come, Peter knew that there was power in what Jesus spoke; therefore, Peter would be able to certainly do what Jesus commanded.

On your journey, you too must stay focused on the assignment, the position, the dream and the passion that has been given to you! Like Peter, life around you can distract you, even though your provider is right in front of you, you still can find yourself taking a look-see at what's going on around you, rather than staying fixed on the way maker. Then just like Peter, you find yourself sinking in the distractions that surround you. Without faith, it is impossible to please the Father. You must remind yourself during this faith walk that there are NO limitations with God. If you doubt what God can do, you are operating in fear. In other words, you are in disobedience.

The reality of the matter is, if you allow doubt to arise, then you are saying that the Father is not almighty, all-seeing, all-knowing, and, most of all, all-powerful. When you find yourself engulfed in fear, confusion, doubt, helplessness, and looking back can become automatic at times, because what's ahead seems scarier than what you are moving away from. Even though Peter had little faith (according to Jesus v.31), he had enough knowledge to recognize he not only needed help, but he realized that Jesus was the one to supply him with that help. Just as Peter had to cry out, "Lord, save me!" you too may need to come to the same realization. When the Father extends His grace through His loving son, He truly saves you and keeps you from taking that moment to glance back.

Now, on the other hand, looking forward displays a boldness that God desires to use. This boldness does not indicate that you got it under control, but it does imply that your faith and trust in God are in place.

Are You Focused To Continue Moving Forward?

Being focused on God means giving up your will and accepting His will as you learn to live out the life that the Father has for you. Rest assured that there is strength in being focused on God. Having a focused view means your perception is on point. When your perception is on point, your view is clear and you tend to walk a bit taller, and your confidence level rises, and that's a great thing.

When you have clarity about the will of the Father concerning your endeavors, all of your senses feel heightened. You love harder, you hear better, and your ability to forgive is even stronger. Let's be clear; you need to ensure that your trust and faith stay in check.

Life, as we know it, has been known to shake some of the strongest men and women in the faith. Be committed to your journey, accepting that the Father is right there helping you ALL the way, one step at a time. When your mind is set on the Father you won't have the desire to look back or stare back. It's like having that same feeling of faith and obedience that Peter had when he first began to walk toward Jesus. If you remember

Peter didn't hesitate to come to Jesus once he called out to him.

With this commitment comes the excitement of the unknown, of what God has in store. This excitement also comes from your faith in knowing the Father as your provider. Knowing that He loves you and desires the best for you makes keeping your eyes on Him a pleasure. But oh, when he took his eyes off of the Holy of Holies, he probably thought as the father in Mark 9:24 (KJV), "Lord, I believe; help thou mine unbelief!" Do you realize the possibility of knowing and still not believing? Have you ever been in that position? Did you find yourself asking for help, as well?

The wonderful thing about the Father, while trying not to look back and being intentional about moving forward, He extends His unconditional love toward you to assist you in the process. He knows your heart and your thoughts, and He still chooses to cheer you on to do your best on this journey of life.

The whole basis of not looking back is all about not missing out on what the Father has waiting for you if you would only walk toward Him and accept what is yours. It's not remaining in a stagnant place because of your past. It is being bold enough to recognize those things are a hindrance and being okay with letting them go for what lies ahead. It's being willing to say 'NO' to some things and some people because you're saying 'yes' to the Father is far greater. It's being mature enough to accept the things of your past, learn from them, and still keep it moving. It's knowing that the Father always has your best interest at heart. It's making the choice to go full throttle, even when you don't have all the specifics.

Again, this walk requires a made-up mind, which will allow you to walk hand and hand with faith, trust, and obedience. These acts are the things that please God. As you continue to make this journey all about "YOU" brace yourself for the journey before you. Are you ready to forge ahead? For those that are still on the fence, what do you have to lose? Come on and experience the love, power, and grace of the Father.

Prayer

Heavenly Father,

I pray that you will give ear to all that concerns me. Father, I need you to strengthen me in this walk. Give me the confidence to know that all things work together for them that love you. Help me to choose you, Father, and help me move away from my past and anything that has become a stronghold and allow me to embrace the wisdom and freedom to follow your lead. Help me, Father, to trust you to do what you have called me to do. On this day, grant me boldness to grow daily in your Holy Spirit. It's in Jesus' name I pray this prayer believing.

Amen, Amen, Amen!

Journal

This is where you take some of that still time and write out how you feel, the questions you have, and allow the Father to heal, mend, and restore your mind.

Journal

Stay the Course

" Let thine eyes look right on, and let thine eyelids look straight before thee. Ponder the path of thy feet, and let all thy ways be established. Turn not to the right hand nor to the left: remove thy foot from evil."

Proverbs 4:25-27 (KJV)

When you think about staying the course, what comes to mind? Is it the fact that staying the course will bring you growing pains? Or is it the fact that you may have to let go of some things and some people that you have grown accustomed to? Whatever your thought process may be, you must be determined to stay the path; you have come too far. You must be ready and willing to choose YOU! While you're on this journey called life, many things will come to play, both good and not so good; and this still holds true if you have made the choice to stay the course. As mentioned in the previous chapter, you must be focused and have a desire to not look back on this journey. What you take in through your eye gate can be dangerous to your course if you are engaged in the wrong stuff. On the reverse side though, if you stay the course and keep your eyes on that which is true and Holy, strength is sure to come.

The things that the Father desires to grow in you are your faith, trust, obedience, and your ability to forgive (sounds familiar, doesn't it). When you chose to commit your situations to the Father it speaks volumes about your trust in Him. It gives you more opportunities to learn from Him. Once you begin to attain these gifts, they will help you maintain hope, even during the most difficult times.

Let's keep in mind that the things we have discussed thus far can only be achieved if God resides in our lives as Lord. Let me throw in this disclaimer, you can achieve things on your own, but the million-dollar question is, will you have peace in it? Will you still serve others in it? Will you have sweet rest in it? When you abide in His will, He will shower you with that insurmountable peace that surpasses all understanding, and this type of inner peace can even be felt in the very midst of turmoil, death, and destruction. After all, He paid the ultimate sacrifice for you to be able to experience this wonderful gift on a daily basis.

Remembering the cross is what will help you to not only stay focused but stay the course as well. Are you at a point in your life where you are tired of going in circles? Then why don't you try following the path led by the Father? Once you taste of His goodness, staying the course will make sense, and He will grant you clarity for the journey. When you stay the course, you will begin to see the growth in the knowledge of the Word of

God take form. Strength and peace are in the Word of God. So let me ask you, how are you maintaining the course? Are you winging it as you go? Are you even on the path at all?

I am aware that issues can come into your life as they do in all of our lives. And yes, these circumstances can make you question the whole God thing, so knowing your path and staying the course may seem far-fetched. And there are those life circumstances that bring devastation and death that can pull you away from the Father instead of drawing you closer to Him.

But let me remind you that the world we live in will always have trouble, pain, suffering, hatred, and disease John 16:33, and it's all due to one thing, SIN! You will never be able to get away from it even in your walk with Jesus. The thing that I desire for you is to sup, dine, or eat if you will, with the Savior. When you dine with someone, you are taking time with that person with the hopes of getting to learn/know a little about them. When you break bread with someone, you begin to share what's on your mind, what's in your heart, and those things that you desire. This is all the Savior wants, an opportunity to pour out to you the love He has and His desires for you to be free from "your" sin.

During this conversation, He wants you to rest in knowing that He is always there for you, even in your pain Psalms 34:18. It's in those times of sorrow He wants to let you know that He will restore you and give you hope again Joel 2:25.

After you give Him the opportunity to dine with you, His hope is that you would be open to surrendering your will to follow His will. Now the common denominator on this journey is...YOU! God has never left the throne, so He is waiting for you to decide if you want to give up all that you are to follow Him.

Keep in mind that staying the course does not eliminate trouble or anything negative from walking that same path right alongside you. What it does is reassure you that the giver of ALL things is with you, and is strengthening you for such a time as this (Isaiah 41:10). So, as you make up your mind to take the first step on this awesome course, fear not. Don't even get weary as you try to keep to the path. You are well informed to "get" on the path and "stay" on the path. Trust what dwells on the inside of you. Stay focused and remember that you may go through some rough patches, not understand some things, and lose some things BUT count it all joy and know that the Father "WILL," not could, not hopefully, not possibly ***restore you***! Because Joel 2:25 (KJV) states, "And **I WILL** restore to you.."

When God speaks a thing, He will absolutely do it. He, my friend, does not lie. These are the promises you have to remind yourself of when on this course. When thinking about staying the course what compels you to not turn back? Is it your children, your mate, your parents, or maybe your career? Any of these reasons are fine, but when you make "YOU" your priority, your desires and dreams should become the center of attention, which then causes you to visualize the course and stay on it. And at this point turning back will not be an option. Your dreams and passions should fire you up daily to stay the course whether you hit the mark or not. This kind of burning fire most definitely sounds like and feels like FAITH, wouldn't you say?

To get on course, and stay the course, faith is inevitable. Faith is what compels you to push past the no's, the unknown, and the losses. Faith says even though a plan is not in place, still trust God. Faith says to do the work even when you don't feel like it. Your feelings should not be a top priority (you should) when it comes to staying the course.

Remember, your feelings can be fickle because they depend on what is going on around you. That may sound like a contradiction, being that you have made the decision to choose you. What I would like to convey is, while on this journey, when you put God first, it will never be about you it will always be about the Father getting the glory 'through' you. Don't you dare forget that someone is waiting for what you have to offer, and your feelings need not be in the way.

Keep the faith and stay the course until your assignment is complete. Remember the thing you named that compels you to not turn back? Keep it in front of your mind, heck hang a picture of it so that you can visually see it daily; it can stir up the boldness you need to step out in faith. What you don't want to do is reject the course God has placed you on because of the uncertainties of life. Doing this signifies that you don't appreciate his gift of faith.

Think if you will, God loves you so much that He grants you the gift of faith, and with this gift, He is loving enough to help you utilize it. So what's keeping you from the course now? What do you need to ensure that you stay the course on this journey?

Is it strength, direction, companionship, financial stability, loyalty, or is it hope? Believe me when I say that all of these needs are very much legitimate. What you don't want to do is allow these things, no matter how valid they are, to rob you from staying the course. Why not introduce yourself to the Father and begin a relationship of a lifetime. As you continue to spend time with the Father you will have a chance to see and know Him as mighty.

Once you realize that He is true to His Word, trusting Him will be second nature even when life happens. So I will ask the question again, how bad do you want this? Are you ready to get rid of the dead weight and get suited in the Word of God? Are you prepared to be persistent and keep your eyes on the Father? Are you ready to love and forgive like never before? Are you ready to grow in your faith? If you said yes to these questions or even have a burning desire to get to your YES, then you are on target and ready to get on course.

Trust that while you are on this course, He is able to use you and work through you to accomplish His will. Don't get weary, but persevere through to the end. It kind of makes you think about the life of Jesus. Even when He knew the fate of His life, He still chose to stay the course and do the will of the Father. Christ's life was not easy. He took up His cross, and He did it, not for Himself, but for YOU. He also asks that you take up your cross if you desire to follow Him. So, are you ready to take up your cross, and walk the walk as you accept the course that has been designated just for you? I implore you to say yes so that you can truly enjoy **Living!**

Prayer

Heavenly Father,

I am thankful for the loving Grace that you extend to me on a daily basis. I thank you Father, for knowing my heart and providing me with the strength I need to stay the course. I pray, Lord that you will continue to stir up what you have placed in me so that I will be able to move in the way you have called me, no matter what comes my way. Thank you Father, for always showing yourself mighty on my behalf. Now, allow me to do the same for others. It's in Jesus' name that I pray this prayer in Hope,

Amen, Amen, Amen!

Journal

This is where you take some of that still time and write out how you feel, the questions you have, and allow the Father to heal, mend, and restore your mind.

Journal

Live in Victory!

> " For the Lord, your God is the one who goes with you to fight for you against your enemies to give you victory."

Deuteronomy 20:4 (NIV)

On this journey, you have encountered many things, both rewarding and challenging. Do you think it is possible to live in Victory? Do you think that you can be victorious when turmoil is engulfing you? The leading scripture should hopefully help you bellow out a strong YES! My desire is that as these circumstances have come and will continue, that you have gleaned something from this reading that will assist you in being ready to live in Victory no matter what comes your way. Have you observed that every chapter in this book is centered on your Heavenly Father? That is because ALL roads lead to Christ.

Living in victory does not, by any means look like, or any way resemble wild-in-out. Living in Victory is a mindset of "I WIN" because of the bloodshed of Christ. This kind of victory has nothing to do with points, status, who you know, or education. Keep reading, you'll see. Here are a few tools to keep on your belt as a reminder to assist you in living victoriously:

1. Surrender

2. Obedience

3. Persistence

The fact that you have continued to read this book shows that you most definitely are persistent.   Let's take a closer look at each of these tools in more detail.

Surrender

Take a look at what is required to surrender. To surrender, one must give up, cave in, back down, or maybe even yield? When I continued to look at the definition, I loved when I read, "cease resistance...and submit to another's authority." (New Webster's Dictionary) Now, to do this type of surrendering, your mind needs to be right remember? (chapter-1) In submitting, you are giving control of "yourself" to someone else, and you must be mentally ready for this.

This means you are willing to stop fighting against the Father's desire and completely submit to His authority. You are relinquishing ALL that you know and understand, over to the Master for Him, to have 100 percent control. So now that you know that this kind of surrendering is expected to live in Victory, do you think it's possible for you to achieve it? You also may be wondering how does this work or what does it look like to surrender? Let me make this very plain for you; you must choose to love you enough to ultimately surrender to God.

Allow yourself time to spend with God. Get in a spot where you can be vulnerable with God, a place where you can be free with God. For me, it's my closet, but keep in mind that the location is not as important as the openness you are about to display before God. This is the place where you will express your most intimate thoughts, your fears, concerns, your desires, and your weaknesses before Him. Once you have located that place, remove anything that may distract your attention (pictures, electronic devices, books, etc.) from focusing on God.

How Should Your Time With God Look?

When you are **ready** to give the Father your time, decide how you want things to flow. Do you want to sing a song of praise first, pray or just be still for a moment? When your mind is on God, you will feel the pull or the desire of what to do. Always follow the Father's lead because He knows what's best. If you are somehow feeling a little uncertain, that's okay. Try singing a song of praise; it helps to usher in the spirit of God. Don't worry about how you sound or if you know all the words. When you sing to God it's a form of adoration, and the fact that it's coming from a sincere and loving place makes it that more special. God knows your heart, and it's beautiful to His ears. Now, take a minute to be still and listen.

The purpose of getting still is to see if the Father wants to speak to you and give you direction, clarity, or just provide comfort. Then, begin to ask for forgiveness of all your mess. Yes, I said mess. We all have it; now give it all to Him. As you continue to pour out to God, be specific and speak these things aloud. When you can hear yourself at this state of yielding, it humbles you even the more, which makes surrendering feel less complicated. As you continue to pour out to the Father, begin to ask Him to take complete control of your life, give Him permission to have His way in your heart, mind, and soul. What you are doing in this process of surrendering is submitting not only your concerns to the Father but most of all every part of "YOU."

This kind of surrendering may seem weary or tiring, but in reality, it brings strength to the believer. This strength is what helps the believer resist the enemy. "Submit yourselves therefore to God. Resist the devil, and he will flee from you." James 4:7 (KJV). How else do you think you can fight against the wiles of the evil one? Surely you didn't think you had this on your own merit.

Obedience

According to the Oxford Dictionary, obedience is listed as "compliance with an order, request or submission to another's authority." It seems that the word submission is something very important, it came up in the surrendering, and now, the obedience section.

When you think about obedience, try and picture the mind of an infant/toddler. They are very eager to please the one taking care of them, right? Right. Therefore, they are very trusting in that same person. They are trusting because they know they must rely on this person for everything, due to the fact, they themselves, are incapable of taking care of their very own needs. So when the one in authority speaks, they generally obey. LOL. When you let go of all you "think" you know, and can do, and decide to trust God at "His" Word, obedience will begin to make sense.

Keep in mind that as good as His Word is, there are times when the **doing** of it may be uncomfortable and scary. This is where you reminisce on the earlier chapters, regarding the importance of establishing a relationship with the Father. When the relationship has been established, the spirit within (Holy Spirit) compels you to do what is right, and if you should fail, stumble, or miss the mark, that same spirit will cause you to quickly repent and begin again.

I believe that when you have a rapport with someone, you are more inclined to do the things they ask and the things that please them. You become loyal because you know and understand their history. You know their desire is to help you, grow you, not cause you harm and despair. Another thing, in order to become obedient, you need to have discipline to do the thing that may seem impossible or even unfair, like forgiving someone that has harmed you. Not very comfortable, is it? I understand because I have been there and had to do that and that is when I realized that our Heavenly Father indeed has a sense of humor.

Let's look at obedience and discipline this way. Consider your current job position. This position comes with responsibilities, whether you like them or agree with them. The discipline, should you accept it, will assist you with walking in obedience to the assignment given to you by your supervisor, because you are aware of the consequences of disobedience. You begin to understand discipline when you don't become combative with those in authority. Learn not to take things personally, even when the situation is personal. Think about it for a moment, the son of God made the noblest act of obedience, even when He really didn't want to, "saying, Father, if thou be willing, remove this cup from me: nevertheless, not my will, but thine, be done" Luke 22:42 (KJV).

As difficult and painful as this act of obedience was, Jesus made a choice to surrender ALL that He had for someone else...YOU! He knew his assignment, and He stayed focused on the end result, not on His current state, especially regarding His own life. That is how you must set your mind. Again, stop taking everything personally because it is not about you, remember, it's about the Father.

Your feelings do matter to God, but they don't necessarily move God. Don't forget He sees all and knows all; therefore, He is very capable of making choices that are beneficial to all involved

Live In Victory

and not get emotionally caught up because then He would be human and not holy. Since your little finite mind can't begin to process all that God is desirous of doing why not just let Him do what He does best.

I know you may be tired of this question but here goes, How bad do you want to live in victory?

- The kind of victory that no matter what, you will obey God's Word.
- The kind of victory that gives way to sweet freedom.
- The kind of victory that understands who the source is and does not fret with the source, does not doubt the source YET takes on the position of rest, full relaxation

in knowing the source as the provider of ALL things.

Persistence

The word Firm is there being very obvious when you examine what the definition of persistence is. But as you continue to read the explanation of persistence, you will see "obstinate in a course of action in spite of difficulty or opposition." BAM! Do you see it? Then the question may arise, what will you need to be firm about when it comes to persistence? Once again, our prime example...Jesus. Is there anyone you know that suffered opposition as He did? NO NOT ONE or dealt with difficulty to the extent that He did? Again, NO NOT ONE.

Yes, you have suffered loss and have been hurt, BUT, what you have never done is live a sin FREE life then chose to die for a world of people who seemed to care less. Persistence is knowing the path before you is a difficult and painful one but still stand firm to move in full pursuit of that path. We talked about passion and purpose early in the book, have you thought about yours anymore? What motivates you or drives you toward your passion? If you are still trying to figure it out, don't forget to create a list of your likes (what you enjoy) and your strengths. After looking over that list look at what you can do to maintain a living doing exactly that. What skills will you need to succeed?

Being able to reach this goal will take persistence. Calls have to be made, research has to be done, and money needs to be in place to see the goal fulfilled. At times persistence will feel like a cycle of failures. When following your dreams/passions, opposition will come and at times back to back. What you have to do is envision that goal daily and remind yourself that someone is waiting for **you** to put it all in place. Set your mind on the finished product, not the building up of it. The mind is a powerful instrument, so visualize yourself doing what's in your heart to do. Allow God to give you clarity, witty ideas, and direction as to what you need to do next.

Your understanding of persistence comes when you never make excuses not to pursue this goal, or you seek ways to get it done no matter the dead ends that may come up. There is a high level of energy that engulfs a person that is persistent. Are you persistent in living your best life? What do you need to put in perspective to become persistent in achieving your goals? The one thing that comes to mind the more I think about persistence, FAITH. I'm sure you have noticed there are certain terms I refer to quite a bit on this road to making it all about you; Faith is one of them. If you reflect on it, faith just fits on this journey. LOL. The reason for this is, if you are going to press toward the mark, you have to believe in the very thing you are pressing toward.

For example, if you desire to be married, you must believe in the attributes of being married, like be honest with your mate, be supportive of your mate, be there for better or worse, be willing to forgive, and the list goes on. You have to be able to dust off or shake off the offenses and still see the ultimate goal in sight, then continue to persist.

When you are persistent, there are opportunities for advancement; in other words, PROMOTION! Think about Joseph; he remained faithful to God throughout all his brothers' hateful tactics. As you know, in the life of Joseph, his persistence paid off. He reaped because he didn't faint. During your pursuit, have you fainted? Or do you feel like fainting now? It's okay if you answered yes. Truth be told, you will get tired, frustrated and sometimes angry; it's natural. But the persistent nature that lies within says, GET UP and get back at it. Now is not the time to sit, rest or give up. There is much to be done and people to serve. What you need to do is listen for the Father to tell you what to do. Have great expectations EVERY DAY!

Believe the Father wants to bless you because of your diligence, for His reward is greater than anything man could ever think to give you. Being persistent is not for the lazy or faint in heart. You must be ready to fight for what you want; otherwise, the vultures will come along and devour the very thing you have worked hard trying to achieve. Stay in position and watch what the Father will do, remember He is a rewarder of them that diligently seek Him. Let me make something clear; when I say stay in position, I'm referring to a mental position. On this journey, you may have to change your physical position when needed. You may have to sit still and listen. You may have to stand watch or even step back a little to get the full view. But your mental position ALWAYS needs to be centered on the Word of God.

Whatever the Father has you to do, just do it because it's in your best interest. In a nutshell, it's like this; step out in faith and allow your faith to assist you in being intentional, and your intentions will cause you to be persistent, and if you maintain your persistence, it will manifest

Live In Victory

itself as a habit. What an awesome habit to have. At this juncture of your life, are you ready to live in Victory? As you prepare yourself to go get 'em, make sure you are ready to die to yourself (surrender) and take on the mind of the Father. Stay emerged in the word of God because that is what will help you stay in obedience. Keep your dream alive and declare His Word over it to help you pursue persistence. After all, the enemy is only waring with you because he understands your gift and Gods' desire to bless you.

Living in Victory is like being born again. You have this daily new task of serving God in excellence, and that should excite you. You understand your role and the role of the Father, and you respect those roles. You have studied the

Word of God, and now it resides on the inside of you. Your gifts have been activated. He has given you everything you need to conquer EVERY giant that comes your way. You have come to the last chapter of this book because you decided to CHOOSE YOU! So guess what, YOU WIN!!! So now go live... in **Victory!**

Prayer

Heavenly Father,

I thank you for accepting me into your arms of protection. Thank you for transforming and renewing my mind. Help me Father, to think on things that are pure, Holy, and true to avoid immoral and impure thoughts. Teach me to live in Victory in every aspect of my life. Help me be ready to die to my flesh so that I may maintain my freedom in you.

In Jesus' name,

Amen, Amen, Amen!

Journal

This is where you take some of that still time and write out how you feel, the questions you have, and allow the Father to heal, mend, and restore your mind.

Journal

www.ingramcontent.com/pod-product-compliance
Lightning Source LLC
Chambersburg PA
CBHW071234080526
44587CB00013BA/1611